Where Does Electricity Come From?

By Angelo Gangemi

Gareth Stevens
Publishing

Please visit our website, www.garethstevens.com. For a free color catalog of all our high-quality books, call toll free 1-800-542-2595 or fax 1-877-542-2596.

Library of Congress Cataloging-in-Publication Data

Gangemi, Angelo.
Where does electricity come from? / Angelo Gangemi.
  p. cm. — (Everyday mysteries)
Includes index.
ISBN 978-1-4339-6315-5 (pbk.)
ISBN 978-1-4339-6316-2 (6-pack)
ISBN 978-1-4339-6313-1 (library binding)
1. Electricity—Juvenile literature. I. Title.
QC527.2.G36 2012
537—dc23
                          2011018184

First Edition

Published in 2012 by
Gareth Stevens Publishing
111 East 14th Street, Suite 349
New York, NY 10003

Copyright © 2012 Gareth Stevens Publishing

Designer: Katelyn E. Reynolds
Editor: Greg Roza

Photo credits: Cover, pp. 1, 7, 11, 13, 15, 17 (both), 21, (pp. 3–24 background and graphics) Shutterstock.com; p. 5 Yo/Stock4B/Getty Images; p. 9 Clive Streeter/Dorling Kindersley/Getty Images; p. 19 Mike Dunning/ Dorling Kindersley/Getty Images.

Printed in the United States of America

CPSIA compliance information: Batch #CW12GS: For further information contact Gareth Stevens, New York, New York at 1-800-542-2595.

Contents

Boldface words appear in the glossary.

What Is Electricity?

Electricity is a kind of energy.
Energy is power used to do work.
Other kinds of energy include heat
and light. We can't see electricity.
However, we can see it work when
we turn on our lights, TV, or computer.

On the Move

Electricity moves through some kinds of matter. It moves very well through **metal**. Copper is a metal used to make electrical **wires**. Electricity doesn't move through some matter, such as rubber. Electrical wires are covered with rubber for safety.

6

copper wire

rubber

7

Electricity and Magnets

A moving **magnet** can create electricity in nearby wires. This works the other way, too. Electricity can be used to make magnets move. Magnets are used in power plants. They turn **motion** into electricity.

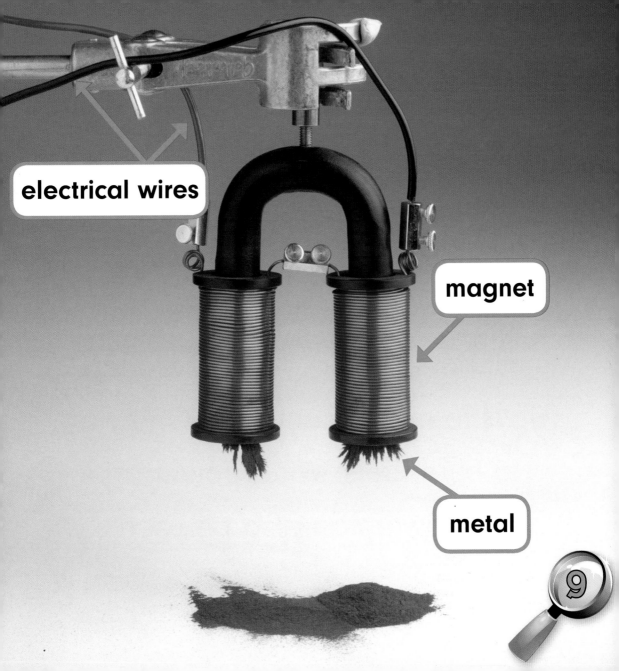

electrical wires

magnet

metal

What Are Generators?

Generators use magnets to create, or generate, electricity in wires. Either the magnets or the wires must be spinning. There are many ways to make them spin. One way is to burn **fuels**. Wind power and water power can also be used.

Making Electricity

Power plants have huge generators. Many power plants burn coal. The burning coal heats water to make steam. The steam spins a giant fan. The fan spins the magnets or wires inside a generator. The spinning motion creates electricity.

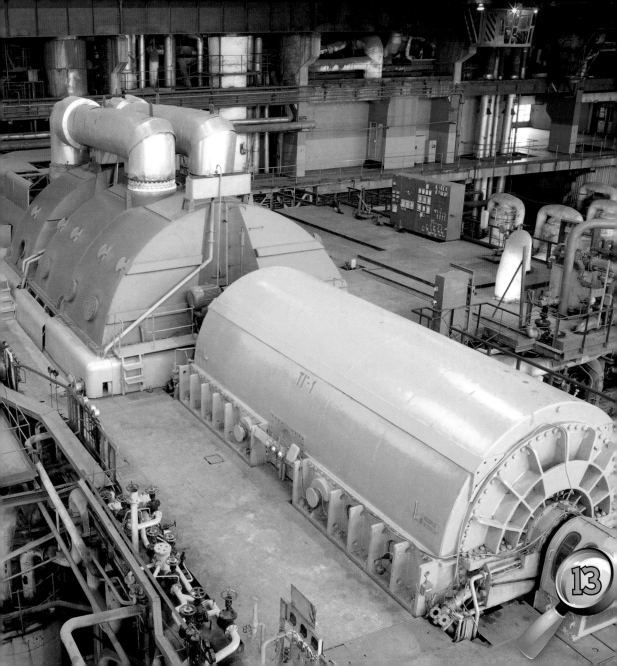

Into Our Homes

Electricity leaves power plants through wires called power lines. Power lines bring electricity to homes. There, smaller wires carry electricity to our lights and outlets. When we plug something into an outlet, it gets the electricity it needs to work.

power lines

15

What Are Motors?

Motors change electricity into motion. In a motor, electricity flows through a wire near magnets. Together, the electricity and magnets produce motion needed to do work. Many objects in our homes have motors, such as fans, tools, and toys.

motor

17

Batteries

Not all electricity is made by generators. Batteries use **chemicals** to make electricity. A battery has two sides called terminals. When a wire is connected to both terminals, electricity flows along it. Can you name something that uses batteries?

18

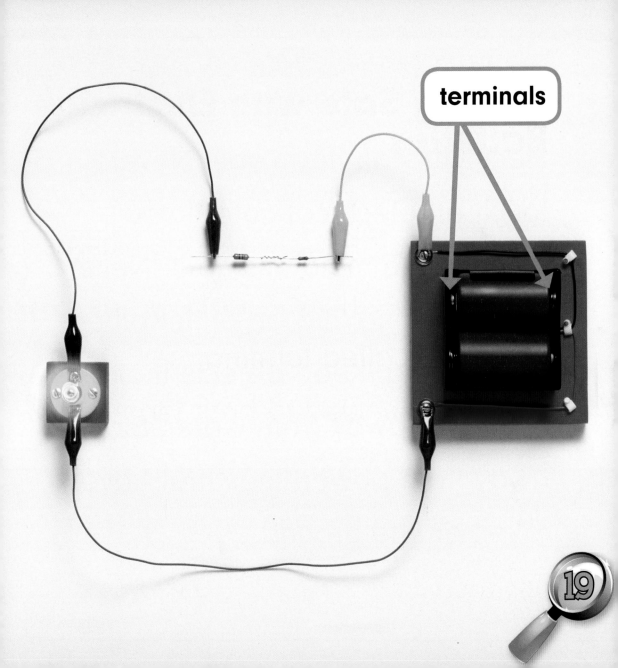

terminals

19

Staying Safe with Electricity

Electricity can harm you. Never touch an electrical cord if you can see the metal inside it. Never stick anything into an outlet other than a plug. Keep objects that use electricity away from water. Stay away from power lines that have fallen on the ground.

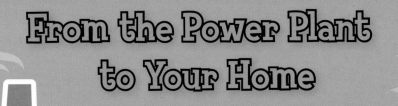

From the Power Plant to Your Home

1. The power plant burns fuel to make electricity.

2. Power lines carry electricity to our homes.

3. Wires in the walls guide electricity to lights and outlets.

4. The electricity powers objects in our homes.

21

Glossary

chemical: matter that can be mixed with other matter to cause changes

fuel: something used to make energy, heat, or power

magnet: something that is able to attract some metals, such as iron

metal: a hard, shiny element found in the ground, such as iron or copper

motion: movement

wire: a thin, hair-like length of metal

For More Information

Books

Royston, Angela. *Using Electricity*. Chicago, IL: Heinemann Library, 2008.

Twist, Clint. *Electricity*. Mankato, MN: NewForest Press, 2011.

Websites

Electricity
www.eia.doe.gov/kids/energy.cfm?page=electricity_home-basics
Read about the use and history of electricity from the US Department of Energy website.

Switched On Kids
www.switchedonkids.org.uk
Learn more about electricity, including safety in the home.

Index